What Do You Know About
Westward Expansion?

PowerKiDS press™

New York

Lynn George

Published in 2008 by The Rosen Publishing Group, Inc.
29 East 21st Street, New York, NY 10010

First Edition

Editor: Joanne Randolph
Book Design: Kate Laczynski

Photo Credits: Cover © Superstock.com; pp. 5, 7–10 (bottom), 13, 15–16, 18–22 © Getty Images; pp. 10 (top)–11 Shutterstock.com; pp. 14, 17 © North Wind Picture Archives.

Library of Congress Cataloging-in-Publication Data

George, Lynn.
  What do you know about westward expansion? / Lynn George. — 1st ed.
      p. cm. — (20 questions, history)
  Includes bibliographical references and index.
  ISBN 978-1-4042-4189-3 (library binding)
  1. West (U.S.)—Discovery and exploration—Juvenile literature. 2. West (U.S.)—History—19th century—Juvenile literature. 3. Frontier and pioneer life—West (U.S.)—History—Juvenile literature. 4. United States—Territorial expansion—Juvenile literature.
I. Title.
  E179.5.G47 2008
  978'.01—dc22
                                              2007031272

Manufactured in the United States of America

Contents

Westward Expansion

The United States has not always been as large as it is today. It began as 13 British **colonies** along the Atlantic coast. Those colonies plus some **territories** made up the United States when it became a free country in 1783. It reached only as far west as the Mississippi River. However, westward expansion continued. Americans believed that God meant for them to have all the land from the Atlantic Ocean to the Pacific Ocean. This belief became known as Manifest Destiny. It changed the lives of everyone who lived there and helped make America what it is today.

This map shows the western states that were added to the Union before and after 1861.

Legend:
- States added to the Union before 1861
- States added to the Union after 1861
- Territories remaining in 1910

1. Do you think 17 are enough?

The United States grew slowly at first. There were 17 states by 1803. However, no new land had been added to the country. The new states had been formed from the territories.

2. We just bought what from France?

The United States bought Louisiana from France in 1803. This was called the Louisiana Purchase. Louisiana was huge. It went from the Mississippi River to the Rocky Mountains and from the Gulf of Mexico to Canada. Suddenly, the United States was two times as big.

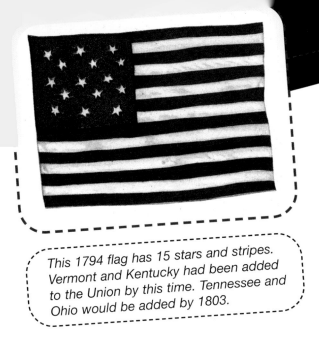

This 1794 flag has 15 stars and stripes. Vermont and Kentucky had been added to the Union by this time. Tennessee and Ohio would be added by 1803.

3. Do monsters live there?

Americans did not know much about Louisiana. Some people thought it might have mountains of salt, mastodons, and 7-foot- (2 m) tall beavers!

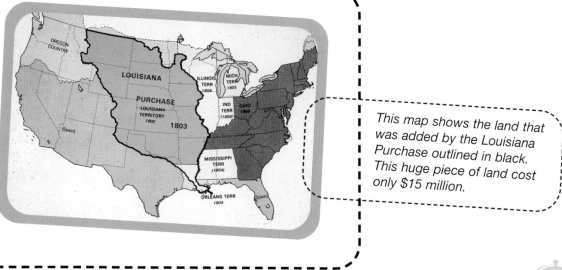

This map shows the land that was added by the Louisiana Purchase outlined in black. This huge piece of land cost only $15 million.

4. What are we looking for?

President Thomas Jefferson formed the **Corps of Discovery** to **explore** Louisiana. He hoped they would find a water path from the Mississippi River to the Pacific Ocean. They never did. However, what they learned about Louisiana's land and people helped settlers.

Thomas Jefferson was born in Virginia in 1743. He is best known for writing the Declaration of Independence, which said that the United States was free from British rule, in 1776.

5. How long will this take?

Meriwether Lewis and William Clark led the **expedition**. They left from Saint Louis, Missouri, in May 1804. They returned in September 1806.

Here Sacagawea speaks to the Chinook Indians to let them know why Lewis and Clark are on their lands.

The only woman in the group was a Shoshone Indian named Sacagawea (sak-uh-juh-WEE-uh). She acted as a guide and **interpreter**. She showed them which plants were good to eat and to treat sickness.

Lewis and Clark hold a meeting with the Omaha and Oto Native Americans at Council Bluffs, Iowa. They likely gave the Native Americans gifts in return for passing through their land.

7. Do you think Mexico will be angry about Texas?

Texas's state flag has a single star on it. This is because the state was once its own country, before joining the Union in 1845.

Many people from the United States had settled in Texas, which was part of Mexico. The American settlers became unhappy with Mexican rule. They said Texas was a free country, in 1836. However, Mexican leaders still considered it part of Mexico. Then the United States made Texas the twenty-eighth state, in 1845. This angered Mexico. The Mexican-American War started, in 1846.

In December 1835, people in Texas started fighting against Mexican rule. One of the most well-known battles during Texas's fight for freedom was fought in 1836 at the Alamo, as shown here.

The United States won the Mexican-American War in 1848. Mexico gave California, Nevada, Utah, most of Arizona, and parts of Colorado, New Mexico, and Wyoming to the United States. Mexico also gave up all claims to Texas.

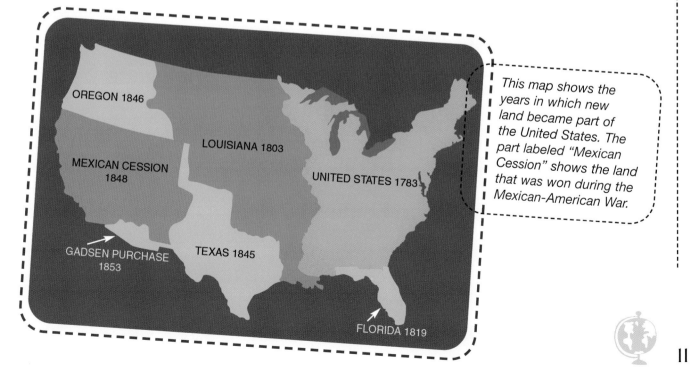

OREGON 1846

LOUISIANA 1803

MEXICAN CESSION 1848

UNITED STATES 1783

GADSEN PURCHASE 1853

TEXAS 1845

FLORIDA 1819

This map shows the years in which new land became part of the United States. The part labeled "Mexican Cession" shows the land that was won during the Mexican-American War.

9. Did you hear they found gold in California?

Gold was discovered in California on January 24, 1848. At that time, there were only about 15,000 settlers in California. Most of them were Mexicans whose families had lived there for many years. That changed after news of the gold discovery spread around the world. Thousands began rushing to the goldfields in 1849. These people came from many countries. They were called forty-niners, in honor of the year.

By 1850, California had enough settlers to become the thirty-first state in the United States. By 1852, more than 250,000 people had come to California as part of the gold rush.

These miners are washing gold in a mining camp set in a river valley during the 1849 California gold rush. Most miners worked hard and found very little gold.

Many people went west on something called the Oregon Trail. The trip was about 2,000 miles (3,219 km). More than 500,000 people went. Some walked the whole way!

This map shows the different paths people took to go west. The Oregon Trail is colored red.

Covered wagons pulled by oxen or mules carried people's belongings. The wagons were called **prairie** schooners because their white tops looked like the sails of ships called schooners.

Here a wagon train makes its way along the Oregon Trail. Most people took up the trail in Iowa or Missouri.

Every day was much the same on the trip west. People woke before sunrise. They ate and then started on the trail. They stopped for lunch. They stopped again about 6:00 P.M. They circled the wagons around their animals, had dinner, and went to bed.

The way west was hard. Families made simple camps, ate bread and bacon nearly every day, and slept on the ground.

Congress passed the **Homestead** Act in 1862 to get people to move west. This law gave 160 acres (65 ha) of land to anyone who lived on the land and farmed it for five years.

On their way to their new homestead, a family stands in front of their wagon in Nebraska. The Homestead Act helped create more than 372,000 farms.

There was no wood on the prairie. Settlers used sod, or blocks of soil and grass, to build houses. They used straw or grass for the roof. Sod houses were warm in winter and cool in summer. However, dirt got in food and on everything. Rats and mice lived in the roof. Snakes and gophers tunneled through the walls and floor.

This picture shows a sod house in Kansas in the 1800s. Once a family had the money, they generally bought wood to make a house.

15. May I please have some fresh vegetables?

Settlers' food was simple. Corn was a basic food for some. It kept well. It could be eaten as a vegetable or used to make bread. **Flour** was another basic food. It did not rot. It was used for many kinds of bread. Meat and dried beans were also important foods. Settlers did not often have fresh fruit or vegetables or milk.

Settlers often had to trade with Native Americans to get the supplies they needed. Here Native Americans and settlers are shown meeting at a trading camp on the Platte River.

Settlers gathered for dancing and singing. They had parties for gathering nuts and **husking** corn. They had house-raisings, at which everyone helped a family build a house. They had horse races and shooting and boxing matches.

This farmer sits husking, or taking the skins off corn, in the 1850s. Corn was a major crop for settlers in the West. People could eat it, and it could be fed to animals, too.

17. Can we take the train?

Westward expansion meant the nation needed a faster way to move people and goods across the country. The government decided to build a **transcontinental** railroad. Work began in 1863 and finished in 1869. Travel from coast to coast now took only a few days.

Here a train passes over a bridge during the building of the Union Pacific Railroad. The Union Pacific was one of the lines of the transcontinental railroad.

18. Did you hear about Idaho and Wyoming?

In 1890, the government said westward expansion was over. Idaho and Wyoming became states that same year. The United States had 44 states.

The United States continued to add states after 1890. Alaska and Hawaii were added in 1959. They were the last states. The U.S. flag then had 50 stars for the nation's 50 states.

Men from the American and Russian governments met to sign papers that said the United States had bought Alaska in 1867. Many American people did not think this was a good use of money.

20. Why are they taking our land?

Here General George Armstrong Custer and his men attack a Native American camp. Custer led a group of U.S. cavalry, or horsemen, whose job was to force Indians off their land to make way for white settlers.

Most people living west of the Mississippi River in 1803 were Native Americans. Some were farmers. Others were hunters who followed herds of buffalo. Others fished and gathered food from the forests.

At first, Native Americans lived peacefully with the settlers. However, they fought back when settlers kept taking their land. Many Native Americans died in the fights or from sicknesses brought by the settlers. Still others died because settlers and the U.S. government killed most of the buffalo. By 1890, the Native Americans were made to live on **reservations**. Their ways of life had been changed forever.

Glossary

colonies (KAH-luh-neez) New places where people move that are still ruled by the leaders of the country from which they came.

Corps of Discovery (KOR UV dis-KUH-veh-ree) The name given to the expedition led by Meriwether Lewis and William Clark to explore the Louisiana Purchase territory.

covered wagons (KUH-verd WA-gunz) Wagons with a top of heavy cloth that is held up by pieces of wood or metal.

expedition (ek-spuh-DIH-shun) A trip for a special purpose.

explore (ek-SPLOR) To travel over little-known land.

flour (FLOW-ur) Wheat that has been pounded into tiny pieces.

homestead (HOHM-sted) A 160-acre (65 ha) piece of public land given by the government to farmers.

husking (HUSK-ing) Removing the outside covering of an ear of corn.

interpreter (in-TER-prih-ter) Someone who helps people who speak different languages talk to each other.

prairie (PRER-ee) A large area of flat land with grass but few or no trees.

reservations (reh-zer-VAY-shunz) Areas of land set aside by the government for Native Americans to live on.

territories (TER-uh-tor-eez) Parts of the United States that are not a state.

transcontinental (trants-kon-tuh-NEN-tul) Going across a continent, which is one of the big landmasses on Earth.

Index

Web Sites

Due to the changing nature of Internet links, PowerKids Press has developed an online list of Web sites related to the subject of this book. This site is updated regularly. Please use this link to access the list:
www.powerkidslinks.com/20his/wexp/